My Hometown Chico
Marcia Myers Wilhite

Published by Marcia Myers Wilhite

Chico, California

Printed in China

ISBN: 0-9741048-0-9

Dedication

This book is dedicated to my husband, Charlie, who has encouraged me throughout this entire project. Without his love, friendship, and support, I would not be the person I am today.

For our children; Charlie II, Sarah, Jaime, Cameron, and Alec. My Chico kids! I love you all so much.

Acknowledgements

My Dad—for your positive spirit and "condensed version" advice.

My Mother—who is in my thoughts daily. I hope she would have been proud.

John and Penny Nopel—I love you both.

Heidi Genasci and Lori Silva—true friends.

My dear family friends from the early days at the University and the original group from my childhood at the Presbyterian Church.

The "old neighborhood" Holben Avenue—so many fond memories!

Historical Restoration/ Photographer/Chicoan: Gary Quiring— for staying mellow while my motivation was constant for one year.

Graphic Designer: Connie Nixon—good friend, who owns the coolest coffee house in town.

Copy Editor: Patrick McCaffrey—your words of wisdom and editing skills have been invaluable.

Chico Enterprise Record: Ty Barbour— your photographic skills and easy going attitude have been wonderful.

Introduction

My Hometown Chico is a special collection of historic and current photographs of Chico, California. It guides the viewer from the Gold Rush days to the simple charm that is Chico today. This combination recreates the experience of a stroll from Chico's beginnings to the still delightful town we know today. *My Hometown Chico* illustrates what makes the city of Chico a unique and special place to live. It shows us why some college students never leave after graduating, staying to marry and raise their children. It also brings an understanding of why many natives return to their hometown to stay.

This is a photographic story of Chico and its people, and how over many generations they have shared this enchanting place, nestled at the foothills of the Sierra Nevada mountains. It reminds us of the richness and importance of Chico's past while encouraging us to be wise caretakers of its current beauty, and mindful of its future.

Looking at the photographs is like opening a time capsule. Together with the written descriptions, it creates a virtual experience as you move from the sights and simple pleasures of yesterday to Chico as it is today. It is hoped that *My Hometown Chico* reflects the city's true character. This book is a photographic remembrance for those who have lived here for many years, as well as for those who have yet to experience my hometown Chico.

1

THE BEGINNING

In 1849 John Bidwell purchased one "undivided half" of Rancho Chico for $1,785. In 1851 he acquired the remainder for $9,000. After a number of additional purchases, John Bidwell's Rancho Chico ultimately totaled some 26,000 acres. During the late 1850s and early 1860, it had become evident to General Bidwell that he should draw up plans for a town on his Rancho as his operations had become quite extensive and people employed in the area needed general services. The initial rush for gold had ebbed and many of the miners were now turning to other pursuits. Bidwell suggested that a survey be made by J.S. Henning, Butte County Surveyor, of a portion of the Rancho, lying between Big Chico and Little Chico Creeks. Under Bidwell's direction, the town of Chico was laid out and the plot plan filed at 11:00 on the morning of December 5, 1860 with the county recorder.

Maine Street (Main Street) became the first street because it had already been used as the primary stage wagon road. The town contained four streets running north and south, each about a half mile in length. Salem and Wall Streets extended from First to Ninth Street. Broadway and Main Streets extended from Big Chico Creek to Little Chico Creek. The cross-streets were numbered from first to ninth, inclusive. Those running east and west were less than a quarter of a mile in length. East of Wall Street was pasture land and west of Salem Street were grain fields.

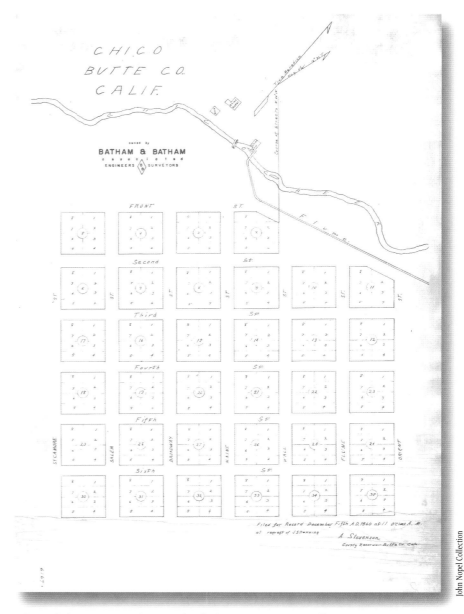

John Nopel Collection

In order to help invigorate the growth of Chico, John Bidwell offered to give lots to anyone who would build. As people began to build homes and businesses it was an exciting time for the small northern Californian town. Early history indicates that the population ratio was about six men to one woman. In the first few years of the little town's existence, there was a great amount of gambling and drinking. Thus, it is not surprising that in 1860 a saloon built on the corner of Main and Third marked the first official Chico building. As the town grew, more families came out from the east to join the working men, creating a much more respectable environment. In 1870 the tremendous growth resulted in the first attempt to organize the town into a city. Although the attempt was unsuccessful, it stirred the minds of Chico's citizenry. In 1872, by an act of the legislature, Chico was incorporated as a city. Various reorganizations have taken place throughout the years, but 1860 and 1872 remain the most significant years in the history of Chico.

OF CHICO

Photo Circa: 1898—John Nopel Collection

Esplanade

Chico's famous Esplanade was traveled by buggies, wagons, bicycles, pedestrians and equestrians. It was the main thoroughfare through Chico on the route from Northern California to Oregon in the late 1800s.

Celebrating fall color along the Esplanade.

The trees that line this historical street in Chico are beautiful year round.

Photo Circa: 1890—John Nopel Collection

Photo: Ty Barbour, Enterprise Record

Photo: Circa 1888—John Nopel Collection

Photo:Circa 1899—John Nopel Collection

General John Bidwell

Born August 5, 1819, in Ripley, New York, John Bidwell spent his boyhood in Drake county, Ohio. A man of remarkable determination, he left home at 17 and walked 300 miles to enroll at Kingsbury Academy. Two years later he was its head master. He arrived in Butte County on horseback in 1847. A little later he traveled more than 90 miles south to work for John Sutter at Sutter's Mill. In 1848 Bidwell was present when gold was discovered at Sutter's Mill in the Sacramento Valley. He became a gold prospector and made a fortune. After 1847 he began making plans to purchase the land that today we know as Chico. John Bidwell was able to acquire almost 28,000 acres using his gold rush earnings. He stocked his land with cattle, horses, fruit trees, and grain. Bidwell thought of himself as a knowledgeable farmer and as Annie's devoted husband. Throughout California and across the nation he was respected as a pioneer, agriculturalist, soldier, statesman, politician, and philanthropist. Active and committed to the very end, General John Bidwell died April 4, 1900 at 80 years of age while he was cutting wood on his estate. He is buried in the Chico Cemetery, next to his wife Annie.

Annie E. K. Bidwell

Like her husband, Annie contributed greatly to the history of California and the development of Chico. The marriage of John and Annie Bidwell was an important event in Washington D.C. Annie was the daughter of the Honorable Joseph Kennedy, who planned the first census of the United States. Present at their ceremony in 1868 were such notable people as President Johnson, General Grant, and General Sherman. After Annie arrived at the mansion that was built in her honor, she named her husband's domain "The Wilderness". It was in the wilderness that she began her life long commitment to not only her husband, but to the Maidu Indians of the Mechoopda Tribe. Annie dedicated herself to improving the educational and employment opportunities for the Indians in the Chico area. She simultaneously taught them her values, which were that of a conservative Christian. After her husband's death in 1900, Annie Bidwell continued to contribute to Chico's prosperity. Besides granting land to the Indians, she also gave Bidwell Park to the City of Chico. On March 19, 1918, Annie Ellicott Bidwell died in the city to which she had devoted 50 years of her life.

Photo: Circa 1868—John Nopel Collection

Photo: Circa 1899—John Nopel Collection

Bidwell Mansion

The kitchen and laundry room are located at the back of the home. The second story contains five high-ceilinged bedrooms, two bathrooms, a servant's quarters and a room which Annie used for sewing and teaching Native American children. A lovely ballroom and six additional bedrooms are located on the third floor which included an additional private office for the General. All of the rooms are filled with exceptional

This elegant mansion was built by General John Bidwell who acquired his wealth during the Gold Rush. It was the headquarters of Rancho Chico, which at one time was the most famous and highly diversified agricultural enterprise in the state of California. The Mansion was a social capital of the West throughout the Bidwells' years together.

Construction of the 26-room mansion began in 1865, which was shortly before General Bidwell was first introduced to his future bride, Annie Ellicott Kennedy. As it became evident that she would become his wife, they planned the furnishings of the Mansion as well as the completion of construction. This Victorian style building was designed by Henry W. Cleveland of San Francisco, who was also the architect of the Palace Hotel. The picturesque mansion was completed in 1868 at a cost of $56,000.00. As you enter the Mansion you encounter a spacious entry hall, a formal parlor, dining room, library, and the General's office.

Photo: Gary Quiring

furniture from the Victorian era. The furniture is of rich, highly polished dark wood, with some marble tabletops. The curtains are made of lace and are delicate to the touch. The fireplaces in many of the rooms are faced with marbleized slate.

The Mansion was used extensively for entertaining the Bidwells' friends and political colleagues. John and Annie Bidwell were well known for their hospitality to the community, as well as to political dignitaries. Some of the elite guests who stayed in the mansion included President and Mrs. Rutherford B. Hayes, General William T. Sherman, Susan B. Anthony, Frances Willard, Governor Leland Stanford, John Muir, Asa Gray, and Sir Joseph Hooker. At the time of her death, Annie Bidwell bequeathed the Mansion and the plush grounds to the College Board of the Presbyterian Church of the United States of America for the establishment of a coeducational Christian school. She requested that Christian values be taught to generations to come. The Church found it impossible to establish such a school. In 1923, the Mansion became the Chico State Teachers College (now known as California State University, Chico). The California State Park System gained possession of Bidwell Mansion in 1964 and it then became Bidwell Mansion State Historical Monument. The title was later changed to Bidwell Mansion State Historic Park.

Bidwell Mansion State Historic Park stands today as a memorial to General John Bidwell and Annie E. K. Bidwell. As the afternoon sun filters through the surrounding trees the beauty of the Mansion is enhanced, and we are reminded of the legacy left to us by the Bidwells.

Deer Park

Annie Bidwell was quite fond of the deer that roamed through the grounds of the mansion. Maintaining a natural environment for the animals, the Bidwell's fenced off an area near their residence which was referred to as Deer Park. It is there that John and Annie spent many mornings feeding and watching the graceful animals.

Maidu Indians of the Mechoopda Tribe

Photo Circa: 1890—John Nopel Collection

Photo Circa: 1870—John Nopel Collection

It is not known exactly when the Indians came to live in Chico, or where they originated. The first residents were part of the Northwestern Maidu Indian group. Their village was located on the south bank of Chico Creek. There were also Maidu villages located in the canyon and near Bidwell Park. While there is no evidence that an Indian village was located directly in the park, a Maidu village, housing the Odowai (Odawi) people, was located near Hooker Oak Five Mile recreation area. The village sites varied in size, some only having a few families, others having over a hundred.

Chico was known for its rich soil and bountiful plants. Wild game and fruiting plants were relatively easy for the Indians to acquire. The Maidu Indians were evidently able to develop a comfortable lifestyle in this area.

First Chico Store

Maidu Indians from the Mechoopda Village pose for a photograph in 1870. They are standing in front of the first store in Chico which was located on the north bank of Chico Creek, near Bidwell Mansion.

Mechoopda Dance House, Chico Rancheria, 1898

General John Bidwell moved the Mechoopda Tribe villages in 1849 to a location approximately three hundred yards southwest of Bidwell Mansion. (Near the present Holt Hall on campus.) He felt that they would be more protected from the destructive transients who sometimes traveled through the area. The Indian men and women performed a variety of jobs on John Bidwell's large estate and received the same pay as other workers on the ranch.

The dance house, hand-made by the Indians, was a large structure, and an important feature on the rancheria. According to an old custom, when a headman died the dancehouse was destroyed then rebuilt by the new leader.

The Indian Church

Built in 1885 by John Bidwell, this simple wood structure became a church for the Maidu Indians from the Mechoopda tribe. Before attending regular services each week at the Presbyterian Church, Annie Bidwell would begin her day teaching the bible to the Maidu Indians at this little church. Soon many from the Maidu tribe wished Annie to perform baptismal, marriage, and burial services. These honors helped Annie Bidwell become an ordained Presbyterian minister in 1889. Each year, on the fourth of July, the Maidu Indians held a fair where they displayed their baskets and beadwork. In the grove outside the church they danced and sang while their brass band played.

The church was destroyed by a brush fire in 1961. It was on the north side of what is today Sacramento Avenue, across from the CSUC soccer field.

Indian Cemetery

The Mechoopda Indian Cemetery is located on West Sacramento Avenue between Mechoopda Street and the railroad tracks. The surrounding area was once part of a village for the Maidu Indians who were of the Mechoopda Tribe. This area is now mostly apartment housing for California State University students. The cemetery was first used in the 1870s after John and Annie Bidwell established "The Indian Church" near the site. The traditional ceremonial rites of the Mechoopda Tribe are still carried out at their burials today. The Mechoopda Tribal Association maintains the 148 ft. by 192 ft. cemetery. Unfortunately, many of the graves are no longer marked due to theft and vandalism.

Photo Circa: 1930—John Nopel Collection

Photo Circa: 1870—John Nopel Collection

Fig Tree

This magnificent tree was located on the grounds of John Bidwell's beloved Rancho Chico, in front of his mansion. It was under its great limbs that General Bidwell sat with many political dignitaries of his time, planning the future of the state of California. Annie Bidwell, with deep regret after the General's death, removed the tree to detour transients who entered the grounds of the mansion to sleep on the shaded benches beneath the tree.

Photo: Marcia Wilhite

The Junction

The Junction was located on 8th Street between Main and Broadway. This was an important transportation center for the teamsters and mining men who worked with the lumber mills that were located on the old Humboldt Road and Butte Creek. It was a mecca of blacksmith shops, stables, corrals, and restaurants that catered specifically to the traveling clientele. This was a hub for saloons, where many men socialized after a long day at work or from a tiresome, dusty buggy ride. A livery stable stood on the corner of 8th and Main Streets until 1912, when it was destroyed by fire. It has been said that "ladies of the evening" had established rooms on the second floor of the Chico Brewery, which was located on the corner of 8th Street and Broadway. With the brewery's close proximity to the Junction, it has been assumed that more than a few of the teamsters and miners may have ventured across the street to their location.

Photo Circa 1920—John Nopel Collection

Photo Circa: 1875—John Nopel Collection

Old Humboldt Road

This Photo was taken about 6 miles north east of Chico. The woman on the far right is Clara Lucas, who was the teacher at Forest Ranch School.

Today, Humboldt Road is designated on road maps as Highway 32. It leads out of Chico on a scenic route to the mountains. As it goes into the foothills, there are stone walls along the roadside that were built in the 1870s. Old Humboldt Road is located to the south of the current paved road. It was used by wagons and coaches. In the late 1800s, lumber was floated down V-flumes in the same area. The historic road was traveled by stagecoaches and wagon trains as they made their way toward the old site of "Fourteen Mile House" where they could be served food and water. The next leg of travel would be toward Forest Ranch, riding the rim of the Iron Canyon of Big Chico Creek, then switching over to the Little Chico Creek rim. Today this route is well loved by sightseers, hikers and mountain biking enthusiasts.

Flume Riders

In 1871 the Chico Flume and Lumber Company built two sawmills at the headwaters of Big Chico Creek. A V-shaped flume was built along the creek which ran all the way to Chico. The flume carried fifty to one thousand feet of lumber to Chico daily. "Riding the flumes" was an exciting and dangerous job. People were hired to float down the flume on timbers to remove debris that might hold up lumber. Many were known to ride the flumes simply for the thrill. Flume Street in Chico was named after the endeavors that took place in the 1870s.

Photo Circa: 1875—John Nopel Collection

11

Street Paving

The first street paved in Chico was on the corner of
2nd and Main Streets.

Bank of Chico

The Bank of Chico was located on the corner of 2nd and Broadway Streets.
The corner location has always been used for financial institutions. Lassen
Savings, Financial Federation, United Savings and Great Western were all
located on the corner. Washington Mutual currently occupies the site.

Town Hall

Chico's first Town Hall was erected in 1872, the year in
which the city was incorporated. It was located on the
east side of Main between 3rd and 4th Streets.

12

Photo Circa: 1911 —John Nopel Collection

Sprinkling Wagon

On hot summer days a water wagon was used to keep the dust down on the streets of downtown Chico. This photo was taken on Main Street in front of the old fire house which was across from the city plaza. A fun summer day activity for many children was to play by the wagon and jump into the misting water to cool down from the Chico heat.

Union Hotel

Chico's first large hotel was the Union Hotel, located at the corner of 3rd and Main Streets. Sadly, it burned to the ground in 1920. This photo was taken in 1905.

Photo Circa: 1908—John Nopel Collection

Train Station

The train station was established in Chico in the late 1800s.

Photo Circa: 1928—John Nopel Collection

Chico Vecino Street Car

Street cars in Chico started running in 1905. This was an innovative and valuable source of transportation for Chicoans during the early to mid 1900s. Sacramento Northern owned all of the street cars that ran through town.

Photo Circa: 1887—John Nopel Collection

Train Wreck

South bound and north bound, California-Oregon Express locomotives collided in 1887. This is what an old time railroader would call "a cornfield meet." Situations like this inspired the saying, "It's a hell of a way to run a railroad!"

Motor Cars on 6th and Broadway

This photograph was taken in 1915 on the corner of 6th and Broadway Streets. Automobiles of this era were both economical and simple.

Photo Circa: 1915—John Nopel Collection

Photos Circa: 1910—John Nopel Collection

Diamond Match Company

Diamond Match Company had a significant impact on the development of early Chico. In 1902 and 1903, the eastern-based company began buying immense stands of timber to establish their first lumber mills in Butte County. In just two years they purchased almost 80,000 acres of trees. The first mill, which turned out 250,000 feet of lumber each day, was built in Stirling City in 1904. The company also built the Butte County Railroad. It erected its Chico mill in 1907. New settlers came to town to work for the mill, contributing to the growth of the town. The labor force had almost 2,000 men in its sawmills, turning out 60 million feet of lumber each year.

The Chico Hotel

The original Chico Hotel opened on New Years Day, 1862. It stood on the land now occupied by the Chico Museum, at the corner of what is 2nd and Salem Streets today. Unfortunately, it was destroyed by a raging fire in 1874. It was later rebuilt. In the late 19th Century the hotel was known as a Chico showplace. There was a private stage coach that was available for use by the hotel guests. The Chico Hotel was massive for its time; a three-story hotel with luxurious accommodations. The hotel was built by Ira A. Wetherbee, at a cost of $24,000. The Chico Hotel and the Union Hotel were the finest of the four hotels in the city during the late 1800s.

Carnegie Library

The first "Free Library and Reading Room" was opened in Chico in 1875. There was an interested group of residents who taxed themselves for the necessary dues. Four years later General John Bidwell generously gave this group a space on the second floor of his 1st and Broadway office building. In 1882 the library moved to a new and more spacious location between 1st and 2nd Streets. An ambitious man by the name of Andrew Carnegie was building many libraries throughout the country and offered his expertise in building a more extensive library that could house more books. The lot at the corner of Salem and West 2nd Street was purchased from a man named Frank Lusk with money donated by private subscription. Mrs. J.L. Morse suggested a plan for the building that was enthusiastically accepted. In March of 1905 the Carnegie Library opened it's doors to the public. In 1939 the building was revised and upgraded with a new wing added. Before its closing to make way for a much larger building in 1982, the library shelved more than 30,000 volumes.

Photograph Circa: 1905—John Nopel Collection

Photo: Gary Quiring

Chico Museum

The historic Carnegie Library Building now houses the Chico Museum. The Mission of the museum is to preserve, exhibit, and interpret the history and culture of Chico, Butte County, and Northern California. Inside the Museum you will find a permanent historical collection on Chico, as well as a featured exhibit that rotates a few times a year.

Photo Circa: 1914—John Nopel Collection

Home Economics Projects

Before 1864, the women of Chico made their own dresses, using only calico or gingham fabric. The ladies always wore sunbonnets; hats were seldom seen. Hoop-skirts became stylish after 1870, and became common apparel for ladies when they dressed for town. This photograph shows home economic projects from a 1914 class.

Photo Circa: 1920—John Nopel Collection

Hannah's Store

Hannah's Store was located at 5th and Broadway in downtown Chico. It was a friendly store that sold general merchandise to the early families of Chico.

Bidwell Store

The Bidwell Store was located at 100 Broadway. This was the first commercial structure built south of Big Chico Creek. The construction of this building was completed in 1861. It was originally a two story building constructed of handmade brick. General Bidwell had his store and office on the first floor; the second floor was used for lodge meetings. Also located on the second story was a "Free Library and Reading Room" for the townspeople. The basement of this building is brick and originally had two vaults which General Bidwell used. The north wall of the present building is the only remaining above ground wall from the original office where John Bidwell spent numerous hours planning the development of Chico. Today, this building houses Tres Hombres Restaurant.

Blacksmiths

The blacksmith trade flourished before the automobile became the primary mode of transportation. The smith and his helpers are pictured next to the forge. This skill is almost extinct today.

19

Butcher Shop

This interesting photograph of a butcher shop in Chico was taken in 1902. The unique carvings on the animal hides were hand-tooled by the butcher. This technique was widely used during this time period to promote sales by beautifying the animal.

Chico Soda Works

The Chico Soda Works was owned and operated by A. Blood in 1870 and was located on 7th and Broadway. It was later moved to the corner of 5th and Ivy Streets in 1895 when the business was purchased by A.G. Eames.

Photo Circa: 1910—John Nopel Collection

The Majestic Theatre

The Majestic Theatre opened to the public in March 1905. It rapidly gained a reputation as a very sophisticated show house. While stopping over on the journey from San Francisco to Portland, some of the finest musical and dramatic troupes of the era performed at the Majestic Theatre. The original seating capacity of 800 included both upper and lower windowed box seats. Originally three stories tall, the second floor was a club and banquet room. The building's owner, the Elks Club, occupied the third floor. This building has since been known as the National, American, and El Rey Movie Theatres.

Bank of Butte County

The first "real" bank in Chico was the Bank of Butte County. Built in 1870, it was located on the corner of 2nd Street and Broadway. The bank was considered the best looking building in town for decades. The bank rented office space on the second floor of their building, one of which was occupied by Dr. Stansbury. Bank of Italy was the next owner, followed by Bank of America, and First Interstate Bank. Chevy's Restaurant chain purchased the building in 1995. It was rebuilt as a Mexican restaurant while maintaining the grandeur of the old bank.

Photo Circa: 1870—John Nopel Collection

Photo Circa: 1920—John Nopel Collection

This photograph was taken from a rooftop in the 1920s, looking down Broadway between 4th and 5th Streets.

21

Richardson Springs

Nestled away in a sheltered canyon just a few miles northeast of Chico is a place that offers serenity and beauty, but unfortunately to very few individuals. Local Indians were the first to discover four mineral springs located in Mud Creek Canyon, which later became known as Richardson Springs. The springs gained a "healing" reputation to the Indians long before movie stars and famous athletes discovered the beauty of Mud Creek Canyon.

Photo Circa: 1910—John Nopel Collection

Photo Circa: 1920—John Nopel Collection

The Maidu and Yana Indians believed that skin diseases, cuts and bruises could be cured by the mud and natural spring water. Because of their strong belief in the healing powers of the springs, the tribes were known to fight

for control of the land. The Maidu Village of Otaki posted lookouts at high points around the springs to keep the Yana Indians away. It was noted that the Indians' daily visits to the springs took on a religious quality.

Reportedly, the first white man to find the springs was Solomon Gore from the Rock Creek area. In 1863, the rancher went searching for lost cattle and came across sulphur smelling water in Mud Creek Canyon. At the time, he had no idea that this water with such an unappetizing smell would bring a historic future.

The land gained its name from the Thomas Richardson family who moved west from Iowa, settling in Mud Creek Canyon in the late 1860s. Brothers Jared and Pierce Richardson established a 5,000-acre cattle and sheep ranch on the property.

Because of the popularity of the mineral water with the Indians, the springs became a local attraction to others that were in the area. The Richardsons allowed the Indians and other settlers to bathe in the waters. Many were known to bring bottles to fill with the "healing" liquid.

Due to the constant flow of people who came to the springs, the Richardsons built a 14-room wood-frame hotel and 25 cottages to accommodate the visitors. This marked the beginning of an exclusive health resort for more than 60 years.

In 1903, the Richardson brothers had advanced in age and divided their holdings among other family members. Joseph Redman Richardson and his wife, Alice, acquired the hotel and springs. A nephew, Lee Richardson, was given half of the property so he could move west and manage the hotel.

The Richardsons began an extensive remodel of the facility in 1919. A fire that swept through the wood hotel in 1921 destroyed their plans. It was replaced with the brick structure that stands today. They slowly rebuilt the resort making it much larger than before. The facility that opened in September 1924, included a 125-room fireproof hotel, a lodge with 27 guest rooms, 50 housekeeping cottages, and 35 sleeping cottages, accommodating almost 600 persons. Included at the resort were a large swimming pool, tennis courts, a massage parlor, and a dining facility.

In the 1920s and 1930s the resort became a peaceful respite from city life for movie stars, athletes, and the Bay area elite. They advertised that you could "Rest, Relax, and Re-Create Yourself!" Fresh milk from their own dairy, a bakery with homemade baked goods, a grocery store and meat market were available to the guests. The resort was rich with entertainment offering first-run movies, dancing, gourmet food, card games, shuffleboard tournaments, horseback riding, and night swimming in the lighted pool.

Photo: Marcia Wilhite

The mineral water remained the strongest draw of the resort. Four springs in all, they were named after different properties of water; Monterey Springs, Iron Springs, Radium Springs, and Sweet Water Springs. The water was in such high demand that it was bottled and sold outside of the resort until World War II.

Business at Richardson Springs Resort declined during the depression. It began to improve during World War II, with not only guests, but soldiers who needed rest, relaxation, and time to recuperate from the war. The addition of slot machines provided a popular pastime for guests.

After the war, business at the springs started to rapidly decline. In 1956 a remodel with modern decor was done in an attempt to revive the once thriving resort. A children's playground and adult recreation center were installed, and a much welcomed bar. By 1957 the resort began closing for winter months, and was then put up for sale. It remained empty until 1968 when it was purchased by Springs of Living Water, Inc., a religious organization that remains at the location today.

Springs of Living Water is a nonprofit organization, and is funded by private donations and conference fees. The organization owns 500-acres along Mud Creek Canyon. Running the conference center is a group called "Youth With a Mission" which is an international movement of Christians from many denominations who are dedicated to training and equipping believers to teach their mission throughout the world. The historic hotel, lodge, and cottages are well kept, though the bottling operation and bathhouse have deteriorated. Sadly, it is believed that the four mineral springs have not been used in many years, and the property is posted with "Private No Trespassing Signs," restricting the beauty of the springs.

St John's Episcopal Church

Before St. John's Episcopal Church was built, Chico residents attended monthly meetings at the Episcopal Mission in the Knight's of Pythius Hall. The Mission, established in 1896, met many times before deciding on a permanent residence for their church building. Mr. A.B. Benton, a church architect, was commissioned to design the new church. Construction of the church was finished in 1905. The structure is made of both brick and wood and is in the Early American Style. There are beautiful stained-glass windows which are still intact. The original location of the Episcopal church was the corner of 5th Street and Broadway. However, in 1912,

Photo Circa: 1905—John Nopel Collection

the U.S. Government purchased this land for the new location of the Chico Post Office, and the church was moved to its present site. Due to the growth of the expanding congregation, in 1986 the worshipers purchased a new, larger site on Floral Avenue, leaving the historic building on Salem Street behind. The Salem Street building was sold and remodeled as a Polynesian restaurant. This caused a controversy among the citizens of Chico. Many people were concerned over the change from a place of worship to a restaurant with a license to sell alcohol. In 1993 the restaurant closed. In 1994, St. Augustine's of Canterbury Episcopal Church bought the historic site and turned the building back to a church where they remain today.

Photo Circa: 1912—John Nopel Collection

Memorial Glass Window

The memorial window that honored John Bidwell was installed in the Presbyterian Church of Chico when the church was located at the northeast corner of Broadway and Fourth Street. It was set in place on Thursday, April 7, 1901. Reverend Willis G. White, Pastor of the Presbyterian Church, presided at the ceremony of consecration. He accepted the gift from friends of John Bidwell who wished the window to be a continuous reminder of this honored pioneer, agriculturalist, philanthropist and humanitarian.

The window was designed by Mrs. Mary Ingalsbe Bradford, a Western artist of distinction from San Francisco. It was constructed by the firm of Ingerson and Glaser of the same city. The opalescent glass used in its design was unique for this time period and exhibited a delicate and intriguing effect not seen in this era.

In planning the memorial window, Mrs. Bradford must have been deeply inspired by this very special man she was to honor. Leaves of the walnut tree are shown in the blue canopy at the top of the window to signify that he was engaged in planting these trees shortly before his death. In the large central panel appear two steep mountain cliffs, and through the gorge between them one would look westward into the distant grain-covered valley below. These mountains represent the strength of John Bidwell's character. Upon the side of the cliff grows a hardy pine tree with its roots grasping the rocks. It typifys his ruggedness as a person. The golden valley suggests the fields where he worked and lived. The sunset sky is emblematic of the West which he loved, the land where he lived and died.

Photo: Marcia Wilhite

The lower panels show symbols which tell more of his life. The shepherd's crook signifies his leadership. The pilgrim's staff and the water gourd remind us of his life as a pioneer. The broken wine glass suggests his belief in work the cause of temperance. The legend which appears at the sides of the lower design reads: "For whosoever shall give you a cup of cold water to drink in my name because ye belong to Christ, verily I say unto you, he shall not lose his reward."

This window is prominently displayed in the main entrance of the Bidwell Memorial Presbyterian Church on First Street. It is a magnificent representation of "John Bidwell ... a man to match God's mountains."

John Nopel Collection

Chico Cemetery

The Chico Cemetery began as a family plot more than 140 years ago. John Bidwell took an active interest in this location and became instrumental in the development of the site as a community cemetery. General John Bidwell and Annie E.K. Bidwell, as well as their relatives and family servants are buried there. The cemetery was historically located on the outskirts of town. Chico has grown to encircle this 35-acre site, positioning it almost exactly in the middle of town. The Chico Cemetery is extremely interesting for its many old tombstones and valuable insight into historic Chico families.

Photo: Marcia Wilhite

Presbyterian Church

The First Presbyterian Church was one of the first churches built in Chico. In 1868, at the first organized meeting for the church General John Bidwell was baptized. The church was built in 1870 with support from Annie E.K. Bidwell, for a cost of $20,000. It stood on the corner of 4th Street and Broadway, the present site of the Waterland Breslaur Building. As the city of Chico grew, it became necessary to move the church from the 4th and Broadway location and build a larger facility to house the growing congregation. Two businessmen, Captain John S. Waterland and Isadore Breslaur, purchased the 4th Street site for what was at the time a relatively large sum of money. Officials in the church then purchased the land at 1st Street and Broadway from Annie Bidwell, and built the lovely brick church that we know as Bidwell Memorial Presbyterian Church.

Photo: Marcia Wilhite

27

Photo Circa: 1888—John Nopel Collection

Inside View

View of the front of the Chico Presbyterian Church auditorium at 4th Street and Broadway.

Catholic Church of Chico

The first Catholic church in Chico was established in 1867. This small church was moved back to make way for a larger structure on the same site in 1908. Among the outstanding features of the present St. John the Baptist Catholic Church are its stained glass windows, all donated by parishioners. These are representative of the life of Christ as depicted in the mysteries of the Rosary and were patterned after similar windows in a church in Italy. In 1928 the church established its present parochial school which was staffed by the teaching sisters of Notre Dame de Namur. The school is on church property, a square block bounded by West 4th and 5th, Chestnut and Hazel Streets.

Catholic Church of Chico, Cal.

Circa: 1868—John Nopel Collection

CSUC Library Tower

An early photograph of the Chico State
Library shows the building in a bare state.
The grounds are not landscaped, and the
rose garden was not established. This
building is currently known as Trinity
Hall, housing the Anthropology Museum
as well as offices and classrooms.

Photo Circa: 1883—John Nopel Collection

Normal School

California State University, Chico, originally named the Normal School, is the second oldest institution in the state university and college system. The city of Red Bluff originally was intended to house this school until John Bidwell stepped in with a generous donation. General Bidwell donated eight acres from his prize cherry orchard to the people and city of Chico for the Normal School. (One cherry tree in his orchard was said to have produced 1,750 pounds of fruit in a single season.) In 1887 the Normal School was established for the education and training of California public school instructors and administrators. In 1889 the first term began with an enrollment of 90 students. A faculty of five, headed by Principal Edward T. Pierce, taught a three-year course beyond the ninth grade. Today, there are 15,000 students. Kendall Hall is the present Administration Building, which was built in 1929 after a horrific fire destroyed the original Normal School Building in August, 1927. CSU, Chico has grown into a picturesque campus, offering academic excellence to students from fifty states and twenty-five countries.

Photo Circa: 1897—John Nopel Collection

CSUC Administration Building/Kendall Hall

Photo Circa: 1829—John Nopel Collection

After the raging fire that destroyed the entire Normal School Building, a 1929 cornerstone was placed atop the original cornerstone of 1889. This stone was to represent the work which lay ahead. The new labor had begun for "more splendid possibilities."

California State University, Chico not only provides its students with a stimulating environment for an education, it also provides the community and visitors with beautiful architecture and centers for cultural growth.

Photo: Gary Quiring

31

Bell Memorial Union

The new BMU was completed in 2001 and is owned and operated by the Associated Students. The building houses the university bookstore, a restaurant, the Union Express, an auditorium, comfortable study areas, a game room, the Information Center and the Associated Students offices.

Photo: Gary Quiring

High School

The first high school in Chico was erected in 1904 and served as a school until 1953. It was located where the CSUC Meriam Library stands today

Photo Circa: 1904—John Nopel Collection

Oakdale School

South of Little Chico Creek, was Chico's second public school. Oakdale was built in 1877. It was a massive three-story structure, of latter-day Gothic style, serving Chico for almost 75 years. Oakdale was torn down in 1950, and the property was later purchased by the University for campus expansion.

Photo Circa: 1890

Salem School

The Salem School was Chico's first permanent school house. The school was opened in 1866, and was located on Salem Street, between 7th and 8th Streets. A senior citizen apartment complex now occupies the site.

Photo Circa: 1866—John Nopel Collection

33

Photo Circa: 1920—John Nopel Collection

Sacramento Avenue School

One of Chico's early schools was located near the crossing of
Lindo Channel, on West Sacramento Avenue.

Photo: Gary Quiring

Language Houses

During the late 1960s and 1970s these homes were owned by different language departments from
the California State University, Chico. The city block of homes was appropriately known as the
Language Houses. Due to the economy, the homes slowly deteriorated and were sold to a private
investor. In the 1990s, the homes were restored to their historic state and rented to students.

Historic Homes of Chico

In the late 1800s, Chico enjoyed a reputation for beautiful homes with spacious lots on tree-lined streets. Chico was renowned for its rich land, clean water, and moderate temperatures. As Rancho Chico developed, the town welcomed hard-working men and women with families. The families had a safe, happy, and healthy living environment with opportunities to build modest but comfortable homes.

The First House in Chico

The owner and builder of the first house in Chico was John James Barham. General John Bidwell gave the lot to Barham, who was the manager of Sperry Flour Mill. Bidwell needed families to build homes in the newly established city of Chico and requested that John and his wife, Arabell be the first to build. Bearing Civil War stamps, the deed for the property was from John Bidwell to John Barham, dated April 13, 1866. The large lot, south of Big Chico Creek, ran from Main Street through to Wall Street. The house was located near the corner of Main and 5th Streets. Today, where the house originally stood, (next to the Senator Theatre) is a mere parking lot. Construction of the historically famous home was completed in 1867, just three years after the Barhams had come to California by ox cart. The house was passed on to their offspring, who occupied the home for over a century.

Photo Circa: 1867—John Nopel Collection

Earll Home

The Earll home, at West 3rd and Hazel Streets, was built in 1879. The home was built for Mr. William Earll, who was active in civic affairs in the Chico community. Mr. Earll was the chairman of the committee that secured the Normal School (California State University, Chico). This magnificent home is of Carpenter Gothic style. The ironwork, wrought in England, tops the roof, gables, and balcony. Although the interior of the home was remodeled during the 1970s as apartment rooms for university students, most of the exterior architecture is still intact.

Photo: Marcia Wilhite

Photo: Gary Quiring

Mansfield House

This Gothic Style house is made of wood and built on a brick foundation. In 1884 Wesley Lee, owner of Lee Pharmacy, had this beautiful two-story house built on the corner of 4th and Flume Streets. It was conveniently located within walking distance of his downtown pharmacy. There are rare stained-glass windows imported from Germany when Wesley Lee built the house. The mansard roof, which was later restored, was one of the first of its kind in Chico. The building is now known as the Mansfield House, after the family who owned the house from 1899 to 1971. The original lot covered over half of the city block. In 1910, Mr. Mansfield's daughter married the son of Dr. N.T. Enloe and the property to the right of the house was gifted to the newlyweds. The lot became the first building site for Enloe Hospital. Indoor plumbing and electricity were added to the house during this same period. The exterior of this house looks relatively the same as it did when it was built. The interior has been remodeled and divided into office space which is leased mostly to mental health professionals.

Photo: Circa 1905—John Nopel Collection

Enloe Hospital

Newton Thomas Enloe, M.D. opened this hospital between 2nd and 3rd Streets in 1913. In 1920, Dr. N.T. Enloe announced publicly that he planned to move his small hospital to a new undeveloped site on the Esplanade. It became evident that patient needs had outgrown the Flume Street location and he felt it necessary to expand. It was noted that $75,000 would be allotted for the construction of the building. It took an extremely long time to materialize. The new hospital between 5th and 6th Streets on the Esplanade was finally completed in 1937. Many architectural expansions and medical treatment advances have taken place over the years.

Enloe Medical Center is a community-owned, nonprofit hospital that provides Chico and the North Valley with emergency medical service and hospital care. Enloe offers a full compliment of health care services available in four separate facilities throughout Chico. It is widely known for cutting edge medical techniques for cardiac care and cancer therapy. Enloe currently offers the most extensive cancer treatment options in the region and opened a full-service Regional Cancer Center in 2002.

Photo: Gary Quiring

Photo: Marcia Wilhite

Stansbury Home

In 1883 Dr. Oscar Stansbury built this classic Victorian style Italianate house for $8,000. His daughter Angelina was born there and remained there all of her 91 years of life. Angelina Stansbury was an art teacher for 40 years at Chico High School. The Stansbury Home is now owned by the City of Chico and administered by the nonprofit Stansbury Home Preservation Association.

Barnard Home

The house was built in 1884 by Dr. C.C. Mason. Dr Mason sold the home to Major Timothy Barnard in 1891. Major Barnard was a civil war veteran, a member of the state legislature, and a prominent business man. Barnard was one of fifteen men who started the movement to locate the Normal School (CSUC) in Chico. After purchasing the house in 1910, Timothy Barnard and his wife Anna remodeled the structure's exterior. They tastefully added a balcony and a covered carriage entrance by implementing the use of unique Greek columns for support. It was bought by California State University, Chico in 1989 and currently houses the CSU, Alumni Association.

Photo: Gary Quiring

Miller Mansion

Modeled after a classic southern style home, Roy Miller and his wife Artie, built their dream house in 1955. The Millers were owners of a grocery store chain in Northern California. They lived in their mansion for over 40 years. Their lush, green gardens were always beautiful and would stop motorists to get a longer look. Cherub fountains, trellises with climbing roses and many flowers spread across the immaculately manicured front yard. A seasonal stream, the Lindo Channel, runs alongside the Miller's garden. Each year during the holiday season, the Miller's would decorate the landscape with bright lights. Also included was an elaborate billboard, lighted with a Christmas greeting which was placed at the front of their property for all to see.

Photo: Gary Quiring

After the Millers died, their grandson, Mike Coen, and his family moved into the mansion, to take on the responsibility of the massive upkeep of the property. Located on the Esplanade, the mansion originally sat on the far northern part of town, though has since been engulfed by the expansion of Chico. The grounds have become difficult to manage. The maintenance has been financially burdening for the Coens and they feel it is not a viable residence for their family any longer. The property has been re-zoned and plans have been made to develop the land commercially. Coen hopes to move the mansion to a more private setting, where he and his family will live.

Photo: Marcia Wilhite

Ninth Street House

Most Chico residents know this charming home on Ninth Street. Chicoans drive by it each day on their way to work, the coffee house, or to go shopping. The front yard of the home is lovely. The colorful flowers change with each season. The bushes are always neatly trimmed, and the walkway always swept. Owners, Dick and Jean Meyer have lived there for 20 years. Dick is usually outside puttering around the garden. A retired maintenance worker from Stanford University, Dick takes great pride in his garden. Chicoans are fortunate to reap the benefit of his hard labor.

Gage Home

This home if built today would be called a "modified colonial." Records indicate that it was one of the first homes built in Chico. The lot was first purchased from John Bidwell by R.H. Allen for a minimal price to help establish a township. Constructed in 1861, there have been few alterations since that time. It is built from sugar pine lumber which was transported by ox team from Hupp's Mill in Paradise. Mr. Allen, a teacher, started a small private schoolhouse in his home in 1862. Shortly after, the town voted a tax to construct the first school building and hired Allen as

Photo: Marcia Wilhite

the principal. Classes were conducted on the second floor of the home until the new school was finished. This designated the building as the first official public school site in Chico. In 1880 the parents of Mrs. Helen Sommer Gage bought the house. Longevity of ownership designated it the "Gage Home" since the house has remained in that family's ownership since. A property management company currently rents the rooms in the house to university sorority students.

Photo: Gary Quiring

The Walker Home

This stately brick home at the corner of Ivy and West Third Streets was built in 1875 by Jefferson Walker, of Walker Brothers Brickyard. His home was one of the few residential buildings in early Chico which was made of brick. The house of Victorian style, includes a Georgian style entrance, of strong proportion and finely laid brick. The Walker family maintained ownership of the home until 1945. It has since then functioned as small apartment housing for university students.

One of the most outstanding walls in downtown Chico is ever-changing. While strolling the sidewalk, one can't help but stop to gaze upon the corner building at 2nd and Main Streets. While waiting for the traffic light, the aesthetic COBA wall is a visual reminder that Chico's art scene is rich with talent. Each month during the summer, five different artists exhibit their work on the outside wall of Zuchini & Vine in the center of downtown Chico. COBA is a volunteer-driven, annual outdoor art exhibit presented by the Chico Art Center, a non-profit arts and education organization.

Photos courtesy of Sal Casa

The Work of Salvatore Casa

A past lecturer of Art at California State University, Chico, Salvatore Casa has lived here for nearly forty years. His paintings have won numerous national exhibitions. His many awards include the prestigious American Watercolor Societies Gold Medal of Honor, for his painting, Studio Wall. By applying an image or word with a reference to art, music, literature, Etruscan wall painting, or his Sicilian heritage, Casa "hopes to convey and provoke emotions and thought through the application of ideas to flat surfaces."

Satava Art Glass

Using ancient techniques to create nature-themed glass vases and sculptures, Richard Satava has been producing vividly colored artworks in his studio since 1977. It is an amazing experience to watch him in action. He designs and blows the glass himself, while running a highly successful wholesale and retail business for his art pieces. His wife Christine, who is also quite artistic, has been instrumental in the success of marketing his product. Satava Art Glass is known for the ethereal jellyfish pieces that are sold throughout the world. Satava's open-air studio, surrounded by a forest of mature black bamboo, is located close to downtown Chico, behind his small retail store. Satava and his crew perform their finely orchestrated glassblowing techniques while listening to vintage rock, producing individualistic art pieces that make this small town business a big city success.

Photo: Gary Quiring

Orient and Flume Art Glass

In 1893 a charming Victorian with a carriage house was built in the historic Oriental section of Chico. Located between Orient and Flume Streets, the house was purchased in 1972 by Douglas Boyd. The property was destined to play not only an important role for Orient and Flume Art Glass, but for the history of Chico. Boyd and David Hopper, both talented young artists, transformed the small carriage house into Chico's first art glass studio. Just one year later, the carriage house studio proved to be too small for this rapidly growing business forcing the two men to purchase a much larger facility on Park Avenue. Early work of the studio was directed toward recreating the silver-luster of iridescent glass produced at the turn-of-the-century by glass artists such as Tiffany, Steuben, and Loetz. This led to their current creations of intricate, three-dimensional design's encased in clear glass. In 1982, Boyd bought Hopper's portion of the business and became the sole owner. The art glass is sold throughout the world in upscale studios. Glass blowing requires a high degree of skill and years of practice. This is the main reason that the company has just a few key artists, who have worked there for many years. Orient and Flume wouldn't be what it is today without Bruce Sillars and Scott Beyers, who are the principal glass blowers. Each has been blowing glass for more than 30 years. Their work is exquisite. Douglas Boyd, the President of the company, is no longer blowing glass. Active in all aspects of the business, he continues to use his talent as an artist in many distinctive ways. Each design that comes from the studio is carefully reviewed by Boyd himself, ensuring the quality of the work. As a new color of glass is developed, or a new design created, he is called upon for his valuable input. In the showroom, which is open to the public, glass is displayed for sale. A museum showing how their glass has evolved over 30 years is located on the premises. Orient and Flume has been shown in prestigious museums including the Metropolitan Museum of Art, Smithsonian Institute, Chrysler Museum, and the Louvre in Paris, France.

Photos courtesy of Orient & Flume

Blue Room Theater

The Blue Room Theater was started by a group of enthusiastic, young theatre artists from Chico. As teens they went by the name of The Cosmic Travel Agency. The five actors created children's puppet shows in libraries, schools, and local cafes. The small theater group began performing for audiences in the backyard of one of the actor's homes and became a recognized name in Chico. After performing their first play at a local jazz club, they began to seriously realize the impact of their success. They packed the house each night with standing ovation audiences. In 1994, they rented the abandoned Masonic Temple, which is located above Collier Hardware in downtown Chico. It was there that the Blue Room Theater was born.

Photo: Marcia Wilhite

Photo: Gary Quiring

Chico Community Ballet

Chico is home to a trove of arts and cultural gems, one of which is the Community Ballet. Each year the company produces several impressive programs which vary from children's productions to advanced ballet artist productions.

Our Hands

The large hands are made of cement and terrazzo with images of Chico embedded in them. Artist Donna Billick created this sculpture in 2000 for the East Plaza of the Municipal Center.

Photo: Marcia Wilhite

Photo: Gary Quiring

44

Photos: Gary Quiring

Downtown Murals

Adding to Chico's uniqueness are the murals that grace almost every large wall downtown. Most of the art is by Scott Teeple, who came to Chico in 1971 to go to school, and like many, remained after graduating. We are quite happy he didn't leave; Chico is a better place because of his talent. An accomplished artist in many areas, Scott is incredibly skilled at painting murals. This can get a bit tricky when one is on scaffolding, at times 70 feet tall.

Graffiti in Chico

In an attempt to eliminate graffiti in downtown Chico, Sorenson's Moving Company sponsored a specific wall outside their building for young graffiti artists. This is a masterful statement that graffiti can be creative and beautiful as its own unique art form.

Photo: Gary Quiring

45

Ringel Park

Chico Artist Jesus Ramirez sees many of his paintings as a "fantastic journey"—the way a dream can be. A native of Mexico, Jesus has lived in Chico since 1978. He has exhibited extensively throughout the United States and several foreign countries, receiving many awards. "Downtown Kaleidoscope" was commissioned by the City of

Chico in 2000, specifically for its 1st Street location. The mural was created digitally, on canvas, using a Teflon coating from DuPont to protect it from the weather. It was bonded to stainless steel and attached to one-inch plywood. Ramirez is yet another Chico artist with phenomenal talent.

Photo Circa: 1860—John Nopel Collection

Seizer, River Boat

River boats have cruised up and down the Sacramento River since 1849. Boats such as the "Seizer" encountered and took care of snags and tree branches which blocked the river. "Seizer" was built specifically as a snag boat and its only job was to travel the river each day removing debris from the water.

Scotty's Boat Landing

Scotty's Boat Landing is famous among locals as well as several generations of college students. It has always been the spot to socialize with friends and relax after a long day in the summer heat, tubing down the Sacramento River, or fishing. Located on River Road, the deck overlooks the Sacramento River.

Tubing

John Scott, a Chico native who owns Scotty's Boat Landing, invited the Guinness Book of World Records to Chico in 1984. By 11:00 A.M. they had counted 16,000 tubers who floated past Scotty's. Reportedly, 60,000 tubers were on the river that day.

Photo: Marcia Wilhite

Photo: Ty Barbour Enterprise Record

1918 Fourth of July Parade

A Fourth of July parade in 1918, marching past the corner at Third and Main Streets.

Roundhouse Ron

Roundhouse Ron has been clowning around for more than 30 years. The face behind this professional clown is Ron Palmer of Chico, who takes his clowning very seriously. Ron has been involved with television and radio in Northern California since 1968. You might find surrounded him by an enthusiastic crowd at Farmer's Market; that is, if he isn't keeping up with his busy clown calender of events through-out Northern California. He has a remarkable talent for creating balloon animals, with a repertoire of 25 in all. Roundhouse Ron is most loved for his ability to make people of all ages laugh.

OLD BROADWAY

Photo Circa: 1928—John Nopel Collection

Senator Theatre

In April 1928, a new theatre with a capacity for 1600 persons opened at 5th and Main Streets in Chico. The owners, T. and D. Jr. Enterprises, who had a string of thirty theatres, built the largest and finest theatre between Sacramento and Portland, Oregon. This prominent building, which occupies almost an entire square block, cost $300,000 to build. In the 1920s and 1930s the stage hosted traveling shows. In the 1940s there were World War II shows, and in the 1960s and 1970s there were rock concerts. It was a popular movie house for over twenty years. The theatre tower was capped by a unique prism which was removed in 1999 due to fears that it might collapse. When the tower was taken down it created a controversy within the community, as the prism was a popular Chico landmark.

Photo: Ty Barbour, Enterprise Record

52

Photo: Ty Barbour, Enterprise Record

Plans for the New Senator

The Senator Theatre Building is currently under an exterior makeover. Owner, Eric Hart, who was raised in Chico, plans to refurbish and restore the tower, prism, marquee, sign, stucco and awnings. Chicoans look forward to the historic building being repainted in colors similar to those dating back to the late 1920s.

Illustration courtesy of Eric Hart

Photo Circa 1954—Courtesy Dino Corbin

Photo Circa 1930— John Nopel Collection

KHSL Radio Station

An application was submitted to establish
the first local radio station for the city of
Chico in October, 1931. It was denied by
the federal radio commission on the
basis that radio stations in the Bay Area
adequately served Chico. In 1935, three
businessmen, Sidney Lewis, Willis
Shields, and Harold Smithson again
applied for a 100-watt broadcasting
licence. Shortly after, Harold Smithson
excitedly announced that their application
had been approved for a 250-watt trans-
mitter and that they would soon open
their studio. This was the beginning of
Chico's first radio station, KHSL.

The Chico Motorcycle Club

The Chico Motorcycle Club lines up in front of the Park Garage before their weekly ride through Chico and the surrounding area. The driver of the motorcycle with the sidecar is Vern Pullins. (Pullins Cyclery) Bill Vandervelden is seventh from the left. Both men were lifelong Chico residents.

Photo: Marcia Wilhite

Collier Hardware

An excellent example of a business and a building that defines downtown Chico is Collier Hardware. The store is a throwback to a different era. From its unfinished ceilings to the thick wooden planks that make up the creaky floor, the tall brick and plaster building has withstood the test of time. In 1871, at the cost of $1600, John Bidwell financed the 1st and Broadway site for the Masonic Lodge, of which he was an active member. They held their meetings on the second floor. For more than 130 years there has been a hardware store on the first floor of this corner building. It has been the home of Collier Hardware since 1935. In 1963 Sylvester Lucena bought 40% of the business, and he became the sole owner in 1971. Today the store is owned and operated by Sylvester and his sons, Marc, Steve, and Matt. Collier Hardware is the true definition of a general store. They have a massive inventory, of which the staff is incredibly knowledgeable. The most modern appliance to the simplest hammer can be found at Collier Hardware. Just as important, though, are the readily available single unit nuts and bolts, something you don't find at many stores today.

55

Photo: Circa 1927
Front Right—Adolph Barth

A. Barth Sporting Goods

The well-known sporting goods store was located at 128 Broadway in Chico. A famous floating fish sign was prominently displayed in front of the store. The 10-foot trout was erected in 1926 and hung above A. Barth Sporting Goods for more than 50 years. Established in 1918, the store was bought by Adolph Barth, from J. Lundquist. The store carried guns, bait, and tackle for more than 60 years. In the 1930s and 1940s they rented bicycles by the hour. It was a hub for many locals who gathered to share their fishing and hunting tales. In 1957, after Adolph's death, his two sons ran the business until it closed in 1986. The trout sign was of interest to many people because of its uniqueness. In 1983, the historic fish was damaged when several college students attempted to steal the sign. They were caught running down Broadway. The fish was repaired and repainted in its original colors by owner Bill Barth. In 1986, the big fish finally got away. It was stolen from the rooftop of the building after the business had closed. Years later, there was an anonymous phone call made to the Barth family home, assuring them it was in good hands. The fish has never been recovered.

56

Photo Circa: 1890—John Nopel Collection

Downtown Saloons

There were many saloons in downtown Chico during the late 1800s. More than 100 years later, this popular pastime in Chico has changed little.

John Konning (second from left) is shown in his Saloon on Main Street between 1st and 2nd Streets. The downtown saloons were a favorite gathering spot for the men of Chico and outnumbered all other retail businesses.

Photo Marcia Wilhite

Photo Circa: 1890—John Nopel Collection

Madison Bear Garden
AKA Lusk Building

The large two-story brick building at the corner of West Second Street was built in 1883 for Franklin C. Lusk. Mr. Lusk was a prominent lawyer, a successful businessman and city official. He used this building as a combination residence and law office. The building was severely damaged by fire in 1932. In 1934, the Annie E.K. Bidwell Parlor #168, Native Daughters of the Golden West bought and restored the site for their club meetings and events. The Golden West ladies had a fine reputation for afternoon teas, where alcohol was forbidden. Before the ladies, Mr. Lusk had been known to use the building for his many social gatherings and late evening parties. Since 1977, Lusk's tradition has been carried on by current owners in The Madison Bear Garden. "The Bear" is also well-known for its social gatherings and spirited events.

Photo: Gary Quiring

57

Sperry Flour Company

In the early 1900s, the Sperry Flour Company had one of the largest milling organizations on the Pacific Coast. The massive brick structure was built by John Bidwell in 1885. It was located on the Esplanade across from Bidwell Mansion, next to where Northern Star Mills is located today. Sperry Flour Company offered stable employment to new settlers in Chico.

In the 1950s, an investor bought the historic building, only to tear it down and build a more profitable apartment complex.

Photo Circa: 1900—John Nopel Collection

Northern Star Mills

The first location of Northern Star Mills was on 16th and Chestnut Streets. Built in 1898, it was used as a feed mill for livestock and bagged grain. The site served as a working mill until 1986 when the building burned to the ground.

R.A. Harelson opened the current location of Northern Star Mills in 1930. R.A. Harelson sold the mill to his son-in-law, John B. Growden Jr., who still owns and operates the business with his son John M. Growden.

Photo Circa: 1920—Courtesy Nothern Star Mills

The young woman is Maribeth Harelson Growden, and the man on the right is R.A. Harelson.

59

Waterland Breslaur Building

In 1902, the Breslaur Estate Company, with Captain John S. Waterland, erected the Waterland Breslaur Building on the corner of 4th and Broadway Streets in Chico. In the early 1900s, the building was the largest business block in the city. Today, it is owned and managed by the Breslaur Estate. The three-story building has been well-maintained and restored. It houses many small businesses, including a few long time local favorites: Chico Paper Company, Cotton Party, and Birkenstock.

Photo: Gary Quiring

Morehead Building

The Morehead Building was built by J.C. Noonan in 1889. It was originally the home of the Chico Meat Company. This gorgeous brick building was purchased by the Morehead Family in 1933. During the 1970s the structure was restored and designed for use as a mall made up of small retail stores. At this time the building's name became "Toad Hall." In 1973 there was a fire which destroyed most of the businesses inside Toad Hall, though fortunately the historic building itself was saved. Today, the building is still under the ownership of a Morehead family member and is called the Phoenix Building.

Photo: Marcia Wilhite

Oddfellows Hall

For sixteen years, the Oddfellows met on the second floor of General Bidwell's office building. At times the space was not adequate since they shared it with the Masons. In 1879, the Oddfellows purchased a lot at 3rd Street and Broadway. Construction of their new hall was completed in 1883. Until 1966, when the Oddfellows moved to a new location, the building contained retail stores on the first floor, medical offices on the second and the Oddfellows Hall on the third. The building has had many uses throughout the years. Most memorable is Lee Pharmacy who occupied the first floor for 112 years. Starbucks Coffee is the current tenant.

Photo: Marcia Wilhite

Photo: John Nopel Collection

Lee Pharmacy

Mr. Wesley Lee poses outside his pharmacy in 1885.

Chinese New Years Parade

Photos Circa: 1890—John Nopel Collection

Chinatowns in Chico

The Chinese made very important contributions to the early history of Chico. They came to California by the thousands in the 1850s, '60s, and '70s. It was believed that in the 1870s there were some 10,000 Chinese existing on the scrapings of the lava beds in nearby Oroville. Chico's "Old Chinatown" was located on Flume Street, between West 5th and 6th Streets in the mid-1860s. By the 1890s the "New Chinatown" had expanded as far as West 8th Street. The early Chinese became firmly entrenched in the town as cooks, vegetable growers, and peddlers. They were also very skilled orchard and laundry workers.

Rock Walls

Most of the locals in Chico know of the rock walls that are in the north and east part of town. They can be seen on Highway 32 east of Chico and along the Airport Road. These walls are an important part of Chico's history. In the 1870s and 1880s, the rock walls were built out of necessity because it was hard to obtain wire for fences. Their use was to create fences to mark property lines and secure livestock. They also enabled farmers to clear their land of the rock making for a much more useful pasture. There have been many heated discussions by local historians about who actually built the rock walls. It is said that the Indians and Swedish built the stone walls by hand in the 1860s. Also mentioned for the construction were the Portugese, while many are under the impression that the Chinese built the walls. Whoever built these historical rock walls would be proud to know that after over 140 years some are still standing.

Table Mountain

Chicoans can find peace and solitude on this unique landmark just outside the city. In the spring, the top of Table Mountain is the perfect place to view the valley and breathe fresh air while surrounded by delightful colors from a variety of wildflowers. California poppies, daisies and lupine create a lush blanket of flowers that can make you feel as though you were in one of Monet's paintings. It is a private retreat only moments away from the city that has been enjoyed for centuries.

Photos: Gary Quiring

63

Photo: Gary Quiring

City Plaza

The oldest part of the Chico City Park system is the City Plaza, located in downtown Chico. This land was a gift from General John Bidwell to the newly incorporated city of Chico in 1872. Many of the trees in the plaza were planted by John Bidwell himself. Some of the stately elm trees remain standing today. At the time that the deed of property was given to the city, General Bidwell requested that it include a clause that the land would be used for a courthouse when Chico became the county seat. Though it is not being used as a courthouse as John Bidwell had intended, we are still able to enjoy this shaded retreat on warm summer days, as well as dance to music performed by local bands during "Friday Night Concerts in the Park."

Photo: Gary Quiring

64

Photo: Gary Quiring

Bidwell Park

The third largest municipal park in the United States, it originally occupied 2500 acres of land. First known as Vallombrosa, the park was part of General Bidwell's Rancho del Arroyo Chico. General and Mrs. Bidwell enjoyed this lush wooded park and sought to preserve and maintain the beauty of its natural state. Their love and appreciation of the area are what prompted Annie Bidwell to donate the land to the city of Chico in 1905 after the General's death.

Since the time of Mrs. Bidwell's gift, the City of Chico has purchased additional land bringing its current size to 3,681 acres. The Park follows Chico Creek nearly 11 miles through the town and into the foothills. The activities in the park are endless. It offers two swimming pools, a golf course, baseball fields, fishing, children's playgrounds, and numerous picnic areas. It consists of two very different sections. The area west of Manzanita Avenue is referred to as Lower Park. It is flat and level with many trails that are enjoyed by runners, walkers and horseback riders. There is an abundance of trees that not only provide ample shade, but a gorgeous array of scenery. The area to the east of Manzanita Avenue is referred to as Upper Park and is located in the Sierra Nevada Foothills. Upper Park remains relatively untouched with majestic canyons overlooking Big Chico Creek. Hikers love the steep terrain that is filled with many natural rock formations. There are exclusive swimming areas that are well known in Northern California for their splendor. It is an absolute mecca for mountain bikers.

One of many memorable events that took place in Bidwell Park was in 1937 when it doubled as Sherwood Forest during the filming of The Adventures of Robin Hood. Actor Errol Flynn was the featured male lead in the Warner Brothers film classic which brought national attention to our city. This technicolor motion picture was first shown in Chico on May 15, 1938. Admission prices were 1 dollar and 10 cents on the first floor, 83 cents and 55 cents in the balcony.

Photo Circa: 1935—John Nopel Collection

One Mile Dam

This photograph was taken in the
1930s at One Mile Dam near
the park entrance. The woman's
swimsuit is indicative of the era.

Photo: Marcia Wilhite

Sycamore Swimming Pool

Sycamore Swimming Pool is located at One-Mile Dam, on Big Chico Creek in
Bidwell Park.

Photo: Gary Quiring

Caper Acres

Caper Acres is a children's playground located east of one-mile recreation area, within Bidwell Park. Swings, tunnels, slides and even a castle with a fantasy theme can be enjoyed by children of all ages. With the beauty of Bidwell Park's old oak trees surrounding the play area, parents find this a wonderful location to spend hours with their children.

Photo Circa: 1890—John Nopel Collection

Photo: Ty Babour, Enterprise Record

Hooker Oak Tree

The famed Hooker Oak was named after distinguished English botanist, Sir Joseph Hooker, who visited Chico in 1877. The Bidwells took him to view the great oak on their property and he proclaimed the magnificent tree the largest California White Oak (Quercus lobata) in the world. Shortly after, Dr. C.C. Parry, an American Dendrologist, proudly referred to the oak as the Sir Joseph Hooker Oak.

Due to the massiveness of its stature, the tree collapsed on May 1, 1977. Ironically, after the fallen tree was examined, it was discovered that its massive size was because it was not really one tree but two trees growing together. Today, in remembrance of the Hooker Oak, stands a monument and a children's playground with an adjoining picnic area.

Cedar Grove

Cedar Grove, located in the heart of Bidwell Park was originally the Chico Forestry Station. The Chico Forestry Station was first established in February 1888 by a grant of land donated by John Bidwell to the State Board of Forestry. Within a short time 29 of the 37 acres of rich soil were planted with native and exotic trees. By March of 1890 more than 15,000 trees had already been planted, with another 30,000 small trees developing in the nursery. These unique and special trees were the subject of research in the 1890s and were eventually distributed or sold to various groups. The State Board of Forestry dissolved in 1893 and the new ownership and management responsibilities were then transferred to the University of California. An extensive survey of the development was conducted in 1918 and 150 different species were documented to be flourishing. In 1921, the Station and adjacent acreage, now known as Cedar

Photo: Gary Quiring

Grove, were sold to the city of Chico. Cedar Grove then became a wonderful addition to the neighboring Bidwell Park and is now regularly used for educational events, such as the annual Shakespeare in the Park performances.

Chico Creek Nature Center

Photo: Marcia Wilhite

The Chico Creek Nature Center is an independent nonprofit organization that was established by the Altacal Audubon Society in 1982. In 1996, the Chico Creek Nature Center separated from the Audubon Society and became its own entity. Located on the south side of Bidwell Park, the center has become a unique attraction for the community, as well as tourists. Chico Creek Nature Center primarily operates as a natural history museum and nature center; it also acts as an information center for Bidwell Park. It has a living animal museum and interactive wildlife exhibits. Chico Creek Nature Center provides excellent spring and summer day camps for children.

Photo: Marcia Wilhite

Bear Hole

Bear Hole, located in upper Bidwell Park, is frequented by high
school and university students throughout the summer.

The History of Pioneer Days

For many years the students on campus and the community of Chico awaited with great anticipation the celebration each year in May, historically known as Pioneer Days. On May 16, 1919, "Senior Day" was instituted to combat low enrollment at the Normal School. A pageant to educate the audience on the Chico community and its history was staged on the banks of Chico Creek. The responsibility of this event eventually shifted from administration to student government. Thus began the famous celebration called "Pioneer Days." The Pioneer Days title was first used in 1927. The name changed for 1 year to "Nepenthe Day," in 1928. The following year it reverted back to Pioneer Days until it was last celebrated in 1986.

Many different activities and entertainment took place as the years evolved. There were baseball games, track meets, dances and variety shows which included faculty members, students and members of the community. One memorable event took place in 1922 when a group was organized by the townspeople for the sole purpose of promoting beard growth. Participants were recognized as the "Whiskerinos." The college soon caught onto this whisker craze and organized their own group of men who grew "a facial fungus" or "cactus crop."

Photos: Circa 1970—Courtesy of The Enterprise Record

In 1929, a student group called the "Grandfather's Club" was organized for the purpose of preserving customs from the old West. The activities of this memorable week included the elections of Little Nell and the Sheriff. Cecile Durbrow was chosen as the first "Little Nell" because she was an outstanding horseback rider. Harold Spencer became the first Sheriff. During the 1960s, Pioneer Week became a week known for partying by university students. Though it was business as usual on campus, many of the students skipped classes to attend social events where drinking was the emphasis. Each year the parties seemed to become larger and visitors who had heard of the event came to Chico to participate in the festivities. During the 1970s and 1980s Pioneer Days tagged the university with its unfortunate party school reputation. The "party town" image heralded the beginning of

the end of the famous Pioneer Days. In 1985 both Playboy Magazine and MTV acknowledged Chico as the place to be for a great party. After two so-called "riots" that took place near university housing, University President Robin Wilson was quoted as saying, "Lets take Pioneer Days out back and shoot it in the head." The last Pioneer Week took place in 1986.

Photo 1986—Courtesy of The Enterprise Record

Photos: Circa 1970—Courtesy of The Enterprise Record

Many have fond memories of the downtown parades, university quad projects on the front lawn of campus, and the sorority and fraternity social events. As with many stories, the tales of Pioneer Week and the parties that took place seem to get larger with time. Pioneer Week will remain a fond memory for those who were able to participate, and is a loss for those who missed out on the town spirit and college fun.

Halloween

On October 31, the streets of downtown Chico come alive with ghosts and goblins from all over Northern California. Halloween in Chico is a monstrous celebration. The majority of the participants are students, but many locals make a point each Halloween to visit downtown to take part in the festivities and view the elaborate and creative costumes.

Photo: Ty Barbour, Enterprise Record

The Chico Rooks

The Chico Rooks are part of an elite mens regional soccer league that has brought highly competitive play to the soccer stadium on the Chico State campus since 1993. Their goal is to provide the North Valley community with the opportunity to play and enjoy soccer at the highest level. The Rooks have been successful in combining local talent with players recruited from out of the area. The strength and success of the Rooks are coupled with strong community support that has allowed the team to attract talented players not only from Northern California but from around the world.

Youth Soccer

Community support for children's soccer is phenomenal. On weekends throughout the year, hundreds of kids ages 4 through 18 can be seen at the 20th Street Park enjoying recreational, competitive league soccer. Shown is a player from Chico's Butte United Soccer, a Class 1, traveling competitive youth soccer club.

Photo: Marcia Wilhite

Photos: Gary Quiring

Cycling around Chico

Chico was voted the number one bicycling town in the nation by Bicycling Magazine.

Mountain biking in Upper Bidwell Park's mountain terrain is known for its exceptional beauty and challenging trails.

77

Photo: Gary Quiring

Silver Dollar Fair

During the last week of May, each year, Chico's community fair takes place at the Silver dollar Fairgrounds. Exhibitors contribute from all over Butte County. The fun includes a carnival midway, a rodeo, auto racing and a nightly concert.

National Yo-Yo Contest

Every fall, expert players from all over the world come to Chico to compete in the National Yo-Yo Contest. The competition is America's premier Yo-Yo contest and it attracts the country's most talented players. Players of all ages display their skills as the sports most respected Yo-Yo Masters judge the top divisions. The event is widely known by Yo-Yo competitors, enthusiasts and local Chicoans. It takes place in the City Plaza located in the heart of downtown Chico.

Photos: Gary Quiring

National YoYo Museum

The National YoYo Museum brings the viewer a historic glimpse into the technical and cultural evolution of the YoYo. The Museum is located inside "Bird in Hand" (which is a fun place to shop) on Broadway, downtown Chico. On display is an exciting collection of one of America's favorite pastimes: YoYos. Eighty years of history and artifacts are shown at the museum including past competition awards. Nostalgic photos of YoYo ad campaigns and tournaments help take the viewer back to the time when the YoYo made its debut in America. The Museum also features the Duncan Family Collection and the Tom Kuhn Collection, which includes the World's Largest Wooden YoYo weighing 256 lbs. The YoYo has been traced back to ancient times and gained popularity in America during the 1920s.

JANUARY

Polar Bear Swim

On New Years Day each year, many Chicoans splash into the new year with confidence, determination and a spark of spontaneity. Although the water feels like ice, some participants have been known to swim naked. The Polar Bear Swim is an annual event that takes place at One Mile Dam in Bidwell Park.

80

Photos: Ty Barbour, Enterprise Record

Wildlife

The Chico area is home to 60% of the waterfowl that migrate through the Pacific Flyway. This "flyway" is the route that millions of migratory birds travel during the summer and winter months. Many different species of ducks and geese gather in the area, making the Chico surroundings their "hometown". The Colusa National Wildlife Refuge, Gray Lodge Wildlife Refuge and the Upper Butte Basin Wildlife area are all just a short drive from Chico. Pheasants can be seen flying above the rich agricultural lands of the valley and several species of quail can be found in the foothills and mountains near Chico.

Bald eagles are known to hunt for prey in the Chico area each winter.

Fishing

Many of Northern California's most famous fishing holes are right here in Chico's backyard. From fly-fishing to secluded clear water streams, including world-class bass tournaments, fishing enthusiasts are surrounded with opportunities that are equal to almost any other area. Horseshoe Lake in Bidwell Park is the site for the world's largest kids' fishing event, "Hooked on Fishing, Not on Drugs." For centuries, the Sacramento River has been a salmon and striped bass fishing site. The foothills west of Chico have a nice string of lakes that hold largemouth and smallmouth bass, catfish, and bluegills. For quiet secluded fishing, the mountains and foothills surrounding Chico and Paradise are laced with many streams. Most of the streams are stocked with trout, while others depend solely upon resident fish.

Photo Circa: 1950—John Nopel Collection

Honey Run
Covered Bridge

The Old Covered Bridge over Butte Creek on Honey Run Road was c[...]
pleted in 1896. The bridge still serves with all but a few of its origin[...]
timbers intact. It is one of the few covered bridges left in California a[...]
the only tri-span bridge in the United States.

82

Sunflowers

Hot summer days may make some people feel wilted, but golden sunflowers thrive under the sun in Chico.

Photo: Gary Quiring

Agriculture

Agriculture in Butte County generates more than $300 million to the local economy per year. The rich soil throughout the area produces a wide variety of crops. More than 10 percent of the total production of almonds in the nation is grown in Butte County. Other substantial crops include rice, walnuts, pistachios, prunes, kiwis, apples, and olives. They are shipped throughout the nation. From mid-February to mid-March an array of tiny flowers bloom in the local orchards. Many look forward to the famous springtime show of blossoms found throughout the Chico area.

Photos: Gary Quiring

Rice Growing

One of Chico's most important agricultural assets is the production of rice. In April or May of each year rice in Chico and throughout Butte County is sown by airplane; over 150 pounds of rice per acre. Rice plants begin to show above the water in which it is germinated three weeks from the time it is planted and is harvested during the fall. Contributing to the success of rice in Butte County is the long growing season, warm summer nights and ideal soil conditions. During the early 1900s, rice was cut and bound into sheaves by horse-drawn binders. Today, it is harvested by self-propelled combines and power equipment. Rice from Butte County is sold throughout the world and is much preferred over rice products from southern states.

Photos: Gary Quiring

Almond Blossoms

Within minutes from downtown Chico you can find yourself amidst beautiful almond orchards. The trees blossom with gorgeous small pink or white flowers during February and March of each year. The nuts are harvested from August to September, and shipped all over the world.

Walnut Trees

The majestic walnut trees throughout Chico bring a peaceful beauty to the town. Not too long ago there were many walnut orchards lining the streets of Chico. It is unfortunate that many have been cut down to make room for development. Fortunately, only minutes from the city you can experience the beauty of walnut orchards along the countryside. The trees do not bloom, but you may notice long yellow catkins during the spring pollination season. Walnut trees are able to self-pollinate since they consist of both male and female parts on the same tree. The nuts are harvested in October of each year.

Photo: Marcia Wilhite

Photo: Gary Quiring

Vineyards

In 1884, a prohibition manifesto was sent by the state Women's Christian Temperance Union to all other unions. Annie Bidwell was an active member of the women's union, leading the fight to ban alcohol. As a result, John Bidwell removed Rancho Chico's abundant vineyards to halt the production of wine. Vineyards have again been planted on the outskirts of Chico and are thriving in the same rich soil where John Bidwell planted his vines more than 100 years ago. The grape vineyards are a welcome addition to Chico's agricultural industry.

Photo: Gary Quiring

Farmers Market

A long-time Chico tradition, local growers put on weekly seasonal produce sales every Saturday in the parking lot at 2nd and Wall Streets in downtown Chico.

Photo: Marcia Wilhite

Shubert's Ice Cream and Candy

Shubert's Ice Cream and Candy is one of Chico's oldest and most loved family businesses. Mr. Leonard Shubert opened this charming ice cream and candy shop in 1938. After his death in 1948, the store was passed on to his nephew, Charles Pulliam who in turn sold it to his son, Charles, in 1980. Shubert's has always been a coveted spot to take your sweetheart for a treat, and has become a Chico landmark. It features mouthwatering homemade chocolates and delicious ice cream. A summer evening ritual for many of the locals is to gather in front of Shubert's and enjoy a tasty ice cream cone with friends or family.

Photo: Gary Quiring

R.W. Knudsen

The R.W. Knudsen Family of natural and organic juices is one of the nations' oldest and best-recognized natural brands. It got its start in 1961 when Russell W. Knudsen started bottling fruit juices from his organic grape vineyard in Paradise, California, based on the belief that his fresh pressed and blended juices should contain only 100 percent natural ingredients, and be sweetened with fruit juice.

Russell's son, William (Bill) Knudsen, became president of the company in 1977 and established a state-of-the-art manufacturing facility in Chico. This allowed the brand to become the leading producer of natural and organic fruit products in the natural foods industry. Bill made a policy of purchasing only certified organic raw materials, which was to lend support to local and national organic farmers. The company was sold to the J.M. Smucker Company in 1984 but maintains the standards and old-fashioned flavor that Russell Knudsen insisted upon.

Today, R.W. Knudsen employs more than 150 employees and is a valuable corporate member of the community. Step into a health food store anywhere in the United States and you are likely to see a Knudsen product. The company is highly regarded by locals and is another unique Chico-based success story.

Sierra Nevada Brewing Company

The highly regarded Sierra Nevada Brewing Company is one of Chico's crown jewels.

As you make your way down East 20th Street you become engulfed by a rich yeasty aroma. It may remind you of freshly baked bread and simmering tomato soup that your grandma used to cook. It is to our good fortune that some of the best beer available anywhere happens to be brewed right here on East 20th Street at the Sierra Nevada Brewing Company. What this means for Chicoans, is that Sierra Nevada's fine ales are on tap in almost every bar and restaurant for a fraction of the price you would pay elsewhere. It also means that if you travel to another city and mention that you are from Chico, someone undoubtedly says, "Isn't that where Sierra Nevada beer is made?"

It all began with Ken Grossman, who was a CSU, Chico chemistry student in the 1970s. In 1976, Ken opened his own shop in Chico specializing in supplying home brewers and winemakers. Each day as he worked in his shop, he dreamed of opening a small brewery.

In 1980, his hopes and dreams became a reality. Ken and his partner, Paul Camusi, opened the Sierra Nevada Brewing Company in a small warehouse in Chico. Their first brewing plant was constructed from old dairy equipment and scrapyard bits and pieces. Their bottling line was from a soft drink manufacturer. By 1987, the high demand for the beer was exceeding the capacity of the small warehouse. It is then that they designed a much larger brewery, which would also would feature a pub and restaurant. The striking facility was built on East 20th Street. The beautiful equipment inside today was also bought "secondhand" as it had been in 1980. The glorious expanse of copper, including the copper-clad control panel, came from a 1960s German brew plant.

Paul Camusi retired in 1997 when the plant reached a peak of 300,000 bottles. That same year Ken began another significant plant expansion.

Ken Grossman is still highly involved with his business, serving as company president. He has a hands-on manner with all aspects of the brewing process, including plant development and equipment maintenance. He can be seen working as a Sushi chef in the restaurant on some occasions, or enjoying an ale with friends at the bar. It is because of his love of music that he most recently built "The Big Room" as a major music and entertainment hall, in the Sierra Nevada building.

Photos: Courtesy of Sierra Nevada Brewery

Chico Brewery

Photo:Circa 1886— John Nopel Collection

The Chico Brewery was established at 8th Street and Broadway in 1886 by Charles Croissant. Croissant intentionally had the two-story brick building built for use as a brewery. He also managed the busy saloon on the first floor. Relatively large for this period in Chico, the building had two rooms on the first floor. The front room was used as a saloon and social gathering spot; the larger room at the rear of the first floor was a working brewery. It has been said that the six rooms on the second floor were occupied by "ladies of the evening." With the active saloon below and the Junction across the street, it is quite probable that the rooms were frequented by more than a few men.

The building has had a diverse past, having been occupied by a number of businesses from a fire hose company to Pullin's Cyclery. Pullin's is still a thriving Chico icon, now located on the corner of 8th and Main Streets. Bustolini's, a fun neighborhood delicatessen, and Iron Mountain Leather, occupy the 8th and Broadway location.

Sierra Nevada Brewing Company produces fine ales and lagers using the highest quality and most natural brewing ingredients. They are rich in flavor, aroma, balance and character. Most famously known throughout the world is the Pale Ale, which has won numerous gold medals. Included in their line-up of fine beers is the Porter, Stout, Wheat, Celebration Ale, Bigfoot Ale and Summerfest. All have been recognized in numerous beer competitions.

John Henry Nopel

John Nopel has a great appreciation for his hometown, Chico. He and I have spent many productive hours together in his cozy home office, crammed full of historic information, discussing our favorite subject: The history of Chico. Tucked away in his file cabinets are his precious photos of Butte County's past. Photographs of his family, awards and certificates he has received, historic data and loving art from his admiring grandchildren make for an incredible collage of memorabilia that cover the walls of his office.

His research and study of local history have been his life long hobbies. He has accumulated an impressive photographic collection of early Chico and Butte County. His historical knowledge of Chico has been a major source of information for me throughout this book. At 88 years of age, his memory is excellent and his historic research accurate. He can speak for hours about his favorite subject, Chico. He frequently presents to local clubs and schools on the history of Butte County. Daily, his telephone rings with someone asking him questions about the history of our hometown, Chico.

A native Californian, John was born in Los Angeles, in 1914, to the late John Henry Nopel and Agnes Bell Nopel. The family moved to Raymond in 1917, and then to Chico in 1919. He attended the Chico Vecino and Central Schools, graduating from Chico High School in 1931, and Chico State College in 1935. He did graduate work at the University of California at Berkeley where he earned a Master's Degree in 1940. He taught elementary school in Anderson, Alameda, and Chico where he became the first principal of Hooker Oak Elementary School in 1948. His next career step was as assistant superintendent of the Chico City Schools. He also served as associate superintendent in the office of the Butte County Superintendent of Schools until his retirement in 1975. He was inducted into the Chico Public Education Hall of Fame in 1994.

John Nopel has been an active participant in many community activities. He is a founding member of the Butte County Historical Society, serving as its president in 1965. He served twice as president of the Bidwell Mansion Association, receiving a special honor from that association in 2001. He is a member of the board of directors of the Chico Museum and served a term on the board of the Association for Northern California Records and Research. He is a member of the California Historical Society, and has been recognized by the Conference of California Historical Societies with an Award of Merit in 1994.

Photo: Gary Quiring

John has been associated with the Bidwell Memorial Presbyterian Church for 84 years. He became a member of the church in 1928, and is an elder and member of the board of trustees. He was the first president of the Chico Area Council of Churches, which was organized in 1956.

John Nopel married his wife Pheleita (Penny) Porter at the Bidwell Memorial Presbyterian Church on August 18, 1940. They celebrated their 60th anniversary of marriage in August 2000. They have three children, four grandchildren and two great grandchildren. Their home is always filled with love from family and friends. I am fortunate to have been able to spend time learning from both John and Penny Nopel.

About the Author

Photo: Gary Quiring

Marcia has loved Chico as long as she can remember. The depth of the feeling for her hometown inspired her to create a book which she felt would capture Chico's memorable sights and stories both past and present. Born at N.T. Enloe Memorial Hospital, on a torrid summer day in July, she has lived her entire 37 years in Chico. She is the mother of two boys, ages two and seven, who were both born at Enloe Hospital. Marcia is an active step-mom to three wonderful children who were raised here. She is married to a kind, talented man, who shares his wife's appreciation for her hometown.

The daughter of a retired Anthropology professor, who taught at CSUC for 35 years, she grew up in Chico during a much quieter time. Her dad often took Marcia to work with him. While he taught a class, she would ride her bicycle on the small trails that curved through the campus grounds and over the wooden bridges that crossed Little Chico Creek. They often discussed the history of the University and the Maidu Indians who had once lived on those very grounds.

Bidwell Park has been precious to Marcia. It is her favorite place to relax. She enjoys running in Lower Park and hiking in Upper Park. Swimming laps at a local sports club is another favorite pastime. Each Saturday she can be seen at Farmer's Market shopping for fresh produce which she incorporates into creative dishes for her family and friends. Photography and gardening have been her long time hobbies along with studying the history of Butte County and the culture of its people.

Colophon

Photography: **Marcia Wilhite, Gary Quiring, Ty Barbour**

Photo Restoration: **Gary Quiring**

Graphic Design: **Connie Nixon**

John Nopel Collection

Bidwell's Avenue, Summer 1898

Bibliography

Association for Northern California
Records and Research
Tales from "Old Hutch"
Chico, California: 1990

Bidwell, John
Echoes of the Past
Sacramento, California: 1974

Boze, M. Jeanne
The Nature of Bidwell Park
Paradise, California: 1991

California Department of Parks
and Recreation
Dear General
*The Private Letters of Annie E. Kennedy
and John Bidwell 1866-1868*
California: 1994

Coleman and Forester
Tailings of Butte Creek Canyon
Sacramento, California: 1972

Guinn, J.M.
Sacramento Valley, California
Chicago, Illinois: 1906

Goni, Mary Compton
Mary Remembers
Chico, California:1990

Hill, Dorothy
The Indians of Chico Rancheria
Sacramento, California: 1978

Hutchinson, W. H.
McIntosh, Clarence F.
A Precious Sense of Place
Published by Friends of the
Meriam Library
California State University, Chico: 1991

Howel-North Books
Butte County, California
San Francisco: 1962

Hunt, Rockwell D.
John Bidwell Prince of California Pioneers
Caldwell, Idaho: 1942

Hutchinson, W. H.
When Chico Stole the College
Chico, California: 1982

Mansfield, George
History of Butte County
Los Angeles, California: 1918

McGie, Joseph
History of Butte County
Chico, California: 1956

Talbitzer, Bill
Butte County, An Illustrated History
California: 1987

Wells and Chambers
Butte County, California
San Francisco, California: 1882

Crowthorne Library
162 High Street
Crowthorne
RG45 7AT
01344 776431

Bracknell
Forest
Council

To avoid overdue charges this book should be returned on
or before the last date stamped above. If not required by
nother reader it may be renewed in person, by telephone,
st or on-line at www.bracknell-forest.gov.uk/libraries

ary & Information Service

5430000082938 1